D0873353

Drama for Students, Volume 32

Project Editor: Sara Constantakis Rights Acquisition and Management: Lynn Vagg Composition: Evi Abou-El-Seoud Manufacturing: Rhonda Dover Imaging: John Watkins

Digital Content Production: Edna Shy © 2015 Gale, Cengage Learning WCN: 02-200-210

Gale
27500 Drake Rd.
Farmington Hills, MI, 48331-3535

ISBN-13: 978-0-7876-9642-9

ISSN 1094-9232

This title is also available as an e-book.
ISBN-13: 978-1-4103-9245-9
ISBN-10: 1-4103-9245-9
Contact your Gale, a part of Cengage Learning sales

representative for ordering information.

Printed in Mexico
1 2 3 4 5 6 7 19 18 17 16 15

Picasso at the Lapin Agile

Steve Martin 1993

Introduction

The first years of the twentieth century were an exciting time. The mechanical age had arrived, the two world wars had not, and the world looked to the future as a time of growth and endless possibility. In *Picasso at the Lapin Agile*, Steve Martin presents an imaginary meeting between Pablo Picasso and Albert Einstein. Twenty-three-year-old Pablo Picasso was well known in 1904, when the play takes place, but a few years away from rocking the art world with the introduction of cubism. Twenty-five-year-old Albert Einstein, a clerk at the Swiss copyright office in search of a publisher for his book *The Special Theory of Relativity*, was soon to change humankind's understanding of the very nature of the physical world. Martin has fictional versions of these two historical figures meet in a very real place—the Lapin Agile is a cabaret that exists to this day at 22 rue des Saules in Paris. They interact with each other and with a collection of exotic locals, discussing the nature of thought, creativity, love, and posterity. And then they are joined by Elvis Presley.

Steve Martin, the playwright, is known throughout the world as a stand-up comic (ranked number six on Comedy Central's "100 Greatest Stand-Ups of All Time") and movie star in dozens of films, from *The Jerk* to *Planes, Trains and Automobiles* to *Roxanne* to *Father of the Bride*. He has written several one-act plays as well as films, short stories, and humor essays. When *Picasso at the Lapin Agile* was produced by Chicago's prestigious Steppenwolf Theatre Company in 1993, it was Martin's first play, and it has remained his only play to gain lasting attention, being constantly in production in local and school theaters around the world.

Author Biography

Steve Martin is known to television and movie audiences as one of America's most famous comedians, with a career in show business that spans decades. He is in fact a Renaissance man, having won several of the most prestigious awards available in American arts for writing for television and movies, acting, comedy, and banjo playing.

He was born in Waco, Texas, on August 14, 1945. His family moved to California when he was five. During his teen years, Martin sold books about magic, a passion of his, at Disneyland. He started college as a philosophy major but then switched to enroll in the theater department at California State University. In 1967, a girlfriend introduced him to Mason Williams, the head writer for the *Smothers Brothers Comedy Hour*. Martin quit college to write for the Smothers Brothers show, winning his first Emmy Award for his writing in 1969.

In the 1970s, Martin wrote for various television shows, including *The Sonny and Cher Hour* and *The Glen Campbell Goodtime Hour*, and performed stand-up comedy, appearing several times on *The Tonight Show*. After guest hosting *Saturday Night Live* in 1976, he became a phenomenon, headlining stadium shows as a stand-up comedian. His comedy albums *Let's Get Small* (1977) and *A Wild and Crazy Guy* (1978) had platinum (one million copies) and double platinum sales numbers, respectively, and won Grammy Awards for comedy.

Martin then became a film star, starting with the title role in *The Jerk* in 1979. He went on to perform in slapstick comedies, such as *The Three Amigos* and two *Pink Panther* films; romances, such as *Roxanne* (for which he won a writing Academy Award in 1987) and *Shopgirl* (based on a novella he wrote); and serious independent films, including David Mamet's *The Spanish Prisoner* and *Novocain*. In all, Martin has appeared in over fifty films.

Martin's first book, a collection of short stories called *Cruel Shoes*, was published in 1977. *Picasso at the Lapin Agile* was his first full-length play; it was first performed in 1993. He also wrote the script for *The Underpants*, a play produced off-Broadway in 2008. He has had numerous humor pieces published in the *New Yorker*.

In 2005, Martin was awarded the prestigious Mark Twain Prize for American Humor. In 2014, he was given an honorary Oscar for his excellence in achievement as a stand-up comedian, musician, and producer. He won a Grammy for Best Country Instrumental Performance for playing banjo on "Foggy Mountain Breakdown," an Earl Scruggs video. In 2013, he released a hit album with Edie Brickell, *Love Has Come for You*, on which he plays fivestring banjo—the title track won the Grammy Award for Best American Roots Song.

Plot Summary

Picasso at the Lapin Agile takes place at the Lapin Agile, a bar in Paris, in 1904. The stage notes for the play explain that this is a year before Albert Einstein was to publish his groundbreaking theory of relativity and three years before Pablo Picasso was to paint *Les Demoiselles d'Avignon*, the painting that would help establish cubism as a new trend in art.

The play opens with Freddy, the bartender, wiping down the bar. Gaston, an older man, enters singing "Ta Ra Ra Boom De Re," an old minstrel-show tune popular in France at the turn of the century, having been performed at the Folies Bergere. Albert Einstein, a twenty-five-year-old physicist, enters.

Einstein explains that he is there to meet a woman. He had arranged to meet her at the Bar Rouge, but he theorizes that there is just as much chance of her wandering into the Lapin Agile as there was of him wandering into the Bar Rouge.

Gaston says that he can describe the woman Einstein is waiting for, because he is an expert about women. Einstein mentions one fact about her —her red hair—and Gaston lists several characteristics of her personality.

When Einstein gives his name, Freddy says that he should not be there. He goes into the audience, takes a playbill, and points to the line where Einstein is listed as the fourth character to appear in the play, not the third.

When Einstein leaves to use the toilet, Germaine, the waitress, comes in. She apologizes for being late. Gaston points out that she was supposed to be the third character in appearance.

Einstein enters, coming through the front door again, repeating that he is looking for a woman he is to meet at the Bar Rouge. Germaine, who was not present earlier, starts to question this, but Gaston tells her not to bother. Instead she asks Gaston if he has seen any good-looking girls, and he describes one he saw the day before.

Suzanne, a beautiful nineteen-year-old woman, enters, saying that she has heard Picasso sometimes goes to the Lapin Agile. When she hears that he might be there tonight, she changes her shirt, telling all of the men onstage except Gaston to look away.

Germaine and Suzanne talk about Picasso, and Einstein asks who he is. Everyone answers at once that he is a painter. Freddy mentions Picasso's interest in blue, indicating his historic blue period, and Suzanne, trying to explain his style, points out the inferior painting over the bar, a realistic rendition of sheep in a meadow. Looking at the painting, Einstein gives his own interpretation of it, emphasizing the idea that the small sheep are overwhelmed by the vastness of the meadow, a reflection on his upcoming theory about atomic movement. Germaine notes that if a painting is only to be interpreted by its meaning and not by its style, then a bad painting and a good painting are equal. Gaston takes this idea further by stating that a bad wine will get him as drunk as a good wine, so asks for a good wine for a bad wine's price. He suggests that this is Einstein's idea with all of his relativism, but Freddy points out that Einstein would not be so clever.

Suzanne passes around a sketch Picasso drew of her. Einstein sees the genius in it; Freddy is noncommittal; Germaine likes it; Gaston admits he does not get it; and Suzanne is disappointed that it does not look like her. Freddy points out that having so many varied opinions makes them a room full of fascinating people, more interesting than people without opinions.

Suzanne explains where she met Picasso. She was coming home and saw him on the stairs of her apartment house. He introduced himself as "Picasso," noting that he had a feeling the name would mean something in the future. He drew a dove on the palm of her hand with his fingernail, and she knew immediately that she would sleep with him. Picasso went to her room; after they had sex, he left. He returned that night with the drawing, saying that he would see Suzanne again. Two weeks later, she is at the Lapin Agile hoping to run into him.

Gaston tells the story of the last time he had sex. He had followed a cat on the street, and it stopped at the feet of a woman about his own age. They went to her apartment. When asked why he only had sex with her once, he explains that she died about an hour later, while he was outside with her cat.

When asked, Suzanne says Picasso views the Lapin Agile as a place where artists go to write manifestos—declarations of their artistic principles. Gaston says that he would like to have a manifesto, to give him a *raison d'e^tre* (French for "reason for being") each morning. Suzanne explains that Picasso claimed to not need a manifesto, himself.

In calculating a bar bill, Freddy asks a math question that Einstein answers immediately. Freddy questions his answer. Einstein explains that he works at the patent office by day, but at night he writes. He is trying to publish his short book, *The Special Theory of Relativity*. Germaine suggests that she might be able to connect Einstein with one of her friends in publishing. When she says it will sell better if it is funny, Einstein says that yes, it is funny. He is not concerned that the book be widely read: he thinks that it could have significant impact in his field if only one person, the German physicist Max Planck, would read it.

Freddy interrupts with another math problem for Einstein to solve. When Einstein answers that easily, Freddy gives him a word problem that combines prices, numbers of bottles of wine, and their dates.

The discussion turns to the new century and the just-ended century. They all agree that the nineteenth century was horrible with noise and pollution. Germaine makes predictions that allude to air travel, the atomic bomb, the information age, and the Beatles. Freddy's predictions are more off-the-mark, concerning wax clothes, the passing phase of the automobile, and the Wright brothers being remembered forever for inventing fudge.

Sagot, an art dealer, enters and says that he recently bought a painting by Henri Matisse, a French painter who, historically, was a friend of Picasso's. When Einstein asks what makes the Matisse painting great, Sagot shows him the picture's frame. It is not, he explains, the frame that makes it great but the boundaries that the artist put on his work. He says that he explained the same thing to Guillaume Apollinaire, a French surrealist poet, but Apollinaire paid no attention.

Sagot talks about how much he will make from selling the Matisse painting. Just by owning it, he has identified it as a worthy work of art. Other dealers from all over the world come to him, he explains, because he knows good art from bad, even though he cannot explain what he sees in either.

Sagot plays a game with Freddy: he has the bartender show him prints of famous pictures and calls out the names of the artists, taking a drink with each correct guess. Then he reveals with each one he guessed he read the artist's signature. Suzanne holds up the drawing Picasso gave her and Sagot is intrigued, offering to buy it from her.

He explains why there are two subjects for paintings that art dealers have trouble selling: Jesus to her when the play is over.

Gaston notes that Picasso and Einstein are both people who will probably change the history of the world, but that such things usually happen in threes; he wonders aloud who the third prominent person in the bar will be. As they are discussing this—Picasso is adamantly opposed to Matisse being the triangle's third point—Charles Dabernow Schmendiman walks in.

Schmendiman introduces himself as an inventor of a rare, inflexible, brittle building material—"Schmendimite"—made from equal parts of asbestos, kitten paws, and radium. He insists that he will be remembered for his work because he is talented, and that, in his opinion, is better than being a genius. He once thought of being a writer, but he created his revolutionary material because he followed his heart. He leaves suddenly when he has a new idea for a tall pointed cap for dunces—the "dunce cap" is actually a symbol that has been used for centuries and is referred to in, for example, Charles Dickens's works.

After Schmendiman leaves, Einstein talks about their effect on history. He and Picasso will not *change* the century, he says, but their work will bend it. His description of how history will be affected sounds like a physics theory about how light is refracted before it reaches the eye, making things like the horizon seem straight when they are not. When Gaston disagrees, they have a shouting match.

Einstein insists that light has mass but then regrets having given away the ending of *The Special Theory of Relativity*. Germaine offers to give a woman's opinion on this, but Einstein points out that gender is not relevant to whether something is or is not scientific truth, referring to Madame Marie Curie, the Nobel Prize–winning physicist who was credited with discovering radium in 1898.

When asked, Picasso says that he is working on an idea. Gaston compares being a painter to the time he painted his gutters, making endless decisions, and Picasso says that it is much like that, except that he makes decisions without thinking about them. Einstein agrees with him about the way ideas suddenly appear.

Asked where ideas come from, Picasso explains that his are from the future. When he describes his process, like his pencil snapping through his paper and into another dimension, Einstein joins in his excitement. Picasso says Einstein could not understand because he is a scientist, but Einstein counters that scientific ideas must be beautiful as well. Picasso recognizes him as a brother. They hug. Germaine cuts through their lofty ideals by suggesting that they got into art and physics to pick up girls, though perhaps unconsciously.

The Countess, the woman Einstein was supposed to meet at the Bar Rouge, enters. She asks Einstein about his ideas regarding gravitational force, and he points out to the others how sexy he finds her. She pays his bar bill, and after noting what a significant night this is in history, Einstein leaves.

Freddy leaves to catch a customer who might leave before paying his tab. He says goodbye to the audience, in case he does not return before the play ends. Gaston leaves to use the toilet, as he has done throughout the play.

Left alone, Picasso and Germaine kiss, revealing that they have had an affair. She chastises him for his womanizing. His artistic talent, she says, makes it possible for him to go from one woman to another. But she says she has been using him, too, to fulfill her fantasy of what an artist would be like. She says that she would just like to settle down with a country boy.

A young female admirer comes into the bar. At first it seems that she is thrilled to find Picasso there, but it turns out that she has mistaken him for Schmendiman. She leaves disappointed. A visitor enters from the back room. He is a singer from the 1950s, clearly modeled on Elvis Presley.

When he calls himself a country boy, Germaine collapses briefly. The visitor explains that he likes to surprise people by showing up unexpectedly, which includes having come to them through time travel.

Einstein and the Countess reenter, surprised to find themselves at the Lapin Agile again. The visitor tells them, when asked, that he sings songs of love. All the people in the bar—Freddy, Germaine, Picasso, Gaston, and Einstein—wish that they could just sing love songs.

Sagot returns to the bar with his camera. They all crowd together to get into the picture. Schmendiman races in to be part of this historic photo, crowding into the front. To get everybody to smile, Sagot tells them to say "Matisse." Picasso cannot smile about this, so they consider another word, eventually deciding on "cheese."

After the picture is taken, the visitor looks at the sheep painting. They are not sheep, he says, they are five women. He has, he explains, been sent from the future with a message from Picasso's muse. As Picasso watches, he waves his hand, and the sheep painting changes into Picasso's *Les Demoiselles d'Avignon*. None of the others notice the transformation. Picasso acknowledges that he cannot paint such a thing yet but tells the others that this is the moment when he leaves his blue period behind.

Asked if he is an artist, the stranger acknowledges that he has known his moment of perfection. They will both be remembered for being originals, Picasso says, even though the stranger reminds him that they both based their art on the art of the Negro (blues and rock and roll in the case of Elvis, and African art in the case of Picasso's cubism).

The set pulls back, revealing the sky. Picasso, Einstein, and the visitor watch a shooting star go by. As they watch, the stars rearrange themselves to spell out their three names—the visitor's name is higher and bigger than the names of the artistic and scientific geniuses.

They all toast the twentieth century, because it will be the century in which the accomplishments of artists and scientists outshine those of politicians and governments. Together, they all improvise a rhyming toast to modernism and their faith in the future, tinged by the visitor's warning that they are entering an age of regret.

The Countess

When Einstein enters the Lapin Agile, he says that he is looking for a woman whom he has arranged to meet at a different bar, explaining that she might show up here because she thinks like he does. Later the woman, identified in the stage notes only as the Countess, actually does show up at the Lapin Agile. She thinks just like Einstein—she understands his bemusement about the cat hitting the closed door, and unlike the other characters, she can converse with him about physics at his own level.

Albert Einstein

At the time of the play, Albert Einstein is a young, twenty-five-year-old unknown, working at the Swiss patent office by day and developing his theories about physics in his free time. He has written a book, *The Special Theory of Relativity*, that does not yet have a publisher, but which audience members know will soon change the world's understanding of physics for all time.

Whereas Picasso, his counterpart in this play, is a sensualist, Einstein is lost in theory. He goes to the Lapin Agile because he is supposed to meet a woman, later identified as the Countess, at the Bar

Rouge: in realistic terms, going to the wrong bar is not the way to find the person you are looking for, but to Einstein, there is as much probability of finding her in one place as there is in the other. In the end, he turns out to be correct; the Countess actually does find him at the Lapin Agile, because she thinks the way he does.

The play shows Einstein to be a mathematical genius, able to do complex math equations in his head in just a moment's time. True to the stereotypes of scientists, he is shy and reserved, holding back his talent without comment. He does, however, defend himself against Picasso, who tries to present science as a simpler task than artistic creation, by showing how the thoughts that he generates and applies to the universe are every bit as creative as anything Picasso is doing.

Female Admirer

Late in the play, a young woman enters the bar and expresses her enthusiasm about seeing "him." Her young enthusiasm seems to mirror Suzanne's infatuation with Picasso, and much is said throughout the play of Picasso's mutual attraction to young women, so it seems that she is there to meet him. As it turns out, however, she is excited because she thinks Schmendiman is there—an unexpected turn of events because everyone else views Schmendiman as a joke and a fool.

Freddy

Freddy is the bartender at the Lapin Agile. He is not an educated man and therefore serves as a foil for Einstein and Picasso as they spin their complex theories about science and art. Sometimes, he likes to tease them for their intellectual superiority, as when he finds out that Einstein is gifted at handling mathematical problems and then proceeds to give him difficult but meaningless word problems to solve. Freddy is dating his waitress, Germaine. He is somewhat jealous of Picasso, with whom she once had an affair, but he is secure in his position as the keeper of the bar.

Gaston

Gaston is an old Parisian man who drinks at the Lapin Agile. He is interested in sex, but only theoretically, acknowledging that his days of sexual activity are in the past. He does, however, remember one woman he had sex with not too long ago, but less than an hour after she was with him she died. He looks nostalgically at the world as it progresses, as it moves out of range of the understandings that he formed when he was a young man. Gaston leaves the stage several times during the play to go to the toilet, because, as he explains, his bladder has become weaker as he has aged.

Germaine

Germaine is the young waitress at the Lapin Agile. She is familiar to the crowd that usually drinks there. Freddy, the bartender, is her boyfriend, and she sometimes has to calm his jealousy.

One of Germaine's most notable moments comes when they are discussing the future and she offers her views of what is to come. Most of her predictions are accurate, as she anticipates air travel, television, computers, and even plastic lawn flamingos, which became trendy in the 1960s, and the popularity of the Beatles. Her prediction that Hiroshima, one of the two Japanese cities devastated by the atomic bomb during World War II, would become a completely modern city is somewhat true, in a twisted way, as is her prediction that cruelty would be perfected in the twentieth century.

When Freddy leaves the stage, Germaine and Picasso discuss the time they had an affair. She accuses him of using her and then forgetting her, but then she says that she used him as well, for the experience of sleeping with an artist. Germaine likes Freddy, but she would really like to be with a country boy. When the visitor arrives and refers to himself as a country boy, Germaine briefly faints, and she has trouble keeping her composure around him after that.

Pablo Picasso

Picasso is the focal point of the play, the character mentioned in the title. He does not arrive onstage until the play has been going on for some time, though he is very much talked about before he gets there. Before he shows up, Suzanne is looking for him because she wants to continue their relationship, which began two weeks earlier. Sagot is looking for him in order to buy his works. Freddy and Germaine and Gaston know him as somebody who comes to the bar frequently.

Picasso has had sexual relations with both Suzanne and Germaine. He treats them, and all of the other women he has relations with, as insignificant and forgettable. Women are inspirations for his art, and he feels that they are lucky to be involved in the artistic process with him, which makes him callous and manipulative toward them. When he seduces women he is acting, not just for himself, but in the name of art.

At the time of the play, in 1904, Picasso is twenty-three years old. He has been in his vaunted "blue period," a time in his artistic career when he painted pictures using almost exclusively blues and greens (a famous example of this is his painting *The Old Guitarist*). Over the course of the play, however, the visitor from the future shows him a painting that he is to do in the future, opening Picasso's eyes to a new artistic vision. Historically, Picasso was to go through a brief "rose period" for a few years before creating *Les Demoiselles d'Avignon*, the painting the visitor shows him. This painting, inspired by African art, was to mark Picasso as a leading proponent of cubism, one of the most revolutionary artistic movements of the twentieth century.

Elvis Presley

See the Visitor

Sagot

Sagot is an art dealer. He has bought and sold Picasso's works before. When he enters the Lapin Agile, he is carrying a small work by Matisse, a colleague and rival of Picasso's, that he recently acquired. Sagot is primarily a businessman, but he also views himself as something of an artist. As he explains it, it is his taste that makes an artwork valuable: if he buys it, then the art-buying public believes that the piece has merit that they do not see in it themselves. He explains the three subjects that he cannot sell paintings of: Jesus, nude men, and sheep.

Sagot returns to the bar late in the play with a camera that he can afford because he makes much more money selling Picasso's works than Picasso makes for creating them. He understands the significance of a night when Picasso and Einstein are in the same place and, with an agent's sense of future value, he wants a record of the evening.

Charles Dabernow Schmendiman

When the people in the bar are talking about how things usually come in threes, they wonder what genius will join them in addition to Picasso and Einstein. Schmendiman shows up. He is not a scientist or an artist, though he once wanted to be a writer. He is an inventor. The substance he created, which he calls "Schmendimite," is not very practical—building codes will only allow it to be used in three cities—and it is not very safe, being composed of asbestos and radium, now known as carcinogens, as well as the paws of kittens. Still, he considers himself to be the peer of Einstein and Picasso because he is a hard worker who follows his heart.

Later in the play, when the bar regulars are having a group portrait taken with Sagot's camera, Schmendiman returns, as if he senses a publicity opportunity. He plants himself in front of the crowd and spreads his arms, to push the others away and draw attention to his presence at this night of geniuses.

Suzanne

Suzanne is nineteen years old and beautiful, one of many young women Picasso has slept with. She arrives at the Lapin Agile hoping to find him. She has a sketch that he made of her, and she fondly remembers their night together. Sagot, the art dealer, offers to buy the sketch from her, but she is not willing to sell it.

When Picasso does show up, however, he does not remember her. He flirts with her again, as if seeing her for the first time. She sells his sketch of her cheaply, just to get rid of it. Later, he recalls their night together in detail, and Suzanne is once more open to pursuing an affair with him, making arrangements to meet up with him after the play.

The Visitor

Late in the play, a visitor from the future comes to the bar. He says that he is there with a message from Picasso's muse, and he reveals to Picasso a vision of *Les Demoiselles d'Avignon*, which will be painted over the course of the next four years and will arguably become the greatest work of the painter's long career.

Although he is only referred to as "the visitor," this character is undeniably based on Elvis Presley, the singer who made a name for himself in the 1950s and went on to earn the title the "King of Rock and Roll." The visitor has the same cultural background as Elvis, being an uneducated young man from rural America with simple, humble manners. He dresses like Elvis, wearing blue suede shoes and expressing an interest in white jumpsuits with big gaudy belt buckles, which became Elvis's signature look later in his career. His speaking manner is peppered with quotes from Elvis songs, including "Blue Suede Shoes" and "All Shook Up." He admits to Picasso that they both took their ideas "from the art of the Negro": Elvis is famous for making rock and roll, a music form derived from the blues of black musicians and popular with white audiences.

The inclusion of Elvis in the company of Einstein and Picasso makes a statement about the significance of pop culture, presenting it as the third point of the triangle with art and science. His talent was more in popular entertainment than in artistic music—more in marketing than in artistry.

Legends

A key for making *Picasso at the Lapin Agile* work is that Pablo Picasso and Albert Einstein are instantly familiar to audience members. They yet have to be introduced to the other characters onstage, and those characters can have doubts about the importance each one of them will have in the future. The people watching the play unfold, however, have no such doubts about these characters' fates. History has proven that Picasso and Einstein were among the most important people in their respective fields, just as they each suspect of themselves.

Topics for Further Study

- Einstein and Picasso, as well as mystery writer Agatha Christie and silent film comic Charlie Chaplin, are all brought together to solve a mystery in 1905 Paris in *Einstein, Picasso, Agatha and Chaplin*, a 2010 novel by Regina Goncalves that is part of her young-adult series about a young time traveler named Caius Zip. Read Goncalves's novel and write an essay about teaching history, focusing on which fictional method you think is more effective: showing historical figures interacting on their own or giving audiences a character like Zip who is like them and can learn about other times along with them.

- Look at a copy of Picasso's *Les Demoiselles d'Avignon*, for which he receives the inspiration in this play. If you did not know that it was one of the pictures that launched a whole movement, cubism, would you be able to see its power? Find or take a photograph of four to six people posed for the camera, then write a comparison of the two images, pointing out ideas Picasso expressed in his art that you think made a difference in the world.

- For this play, Steve Martin includes

a selection of predictions for the future of the twentieth century that are comic because they are ridiculous. Make your own list of ten or more ridiculous predictions for the twenty-first century. After each one of them, write a brief explanation about how it could come true but why you think it really will not, drawing on science, history, religion, and politics as appropriate.

- Science marches on. Research the big names in physics who have not yet won a Nobel Prize for their work. Split into teams that will make their cases using multimedia presentations to your class for candidates in a class-wide election for who should win the prize next and why.

- *Harriet Tubman Visits a Therapist* is a 2011 play written by Carolyn Gage. In it, Gage, like Martin, places a historical figure in an imagined situation: in this case Tubman, a key figure in the Underground Railroad during the Civil War, is sentenced to therapy. Read Gage's play after reading Martin's, and then lead a class discussion about the ways that fictional alternate histories help people understand the realities of their world.

- Listen to the music of Elvis Presley, the obvious inspiration for the visitor in this play. Write a song in Elvis's style about this night at the Lapin Agile. Then write an explanation of the song that tells readers not only the events that are referred to but also the way that the music's style is the right way of conveying those events.

- Write your own short, one-act fantasy play about a historic meeting of several famous people you think were most important in the 1970s, 1980s, or 1990s. Make sure to place this meeting in a setting that you think will be evocative of the time, such as a disco or a coffee shop.

The legendary status of those two characters makes them recognizable when their names are evoked. The play's thinly disguised visitor, Elvis Presley, has a personal style that was so distinct that audience members born decades after Elvis's death will recognize his mannerisms. This further gives the play a preexisting context. Audiences come to the performance with ideas about who these men were and what they stood for. Some of their actions onstage conform to these expectations and others diverge from them, which helps to make the play constantly interesting.

Art and Society

Many ideas are explored in this play, but Martin seems to focus particularly on the relationship between the artist and society. Pablo Picasso is portrayed as a callous womanizer, but the play questions how much of that attitude is caused by his personality and how much is due to his immense artistic talent. When he arrives onstage, he has just completed an afternoon of productive sketching. At the Lapin Agile, the patrons who appreciate his talent, such as Suzanne and Sagot and, to some extent, Germaine, accept his arrogance because they know what a great artist he is. They recognize that his artistic drive is more important than the discomfort that his sexist, egotistical behavior causes them.

Even though the gifted artist is an important figure within the space of this small Parisian bar, he does not mean all that much to the world outside its doors. The presence of Sagot, the art dealer, helps put Picasso in his place. Although Picasso is the artist, it is Sagot's genius for identifying and marketing his pictures that the world really pays for, which is why he is rich and Picasso is not. Later in the play Martin brings in a popular musician based on Elvis Presley to show that, in the eyes of society, the ability to deliver catchy lyrics in an entertaining way is at least as important as the skill of a truly gifted artist.

Popular Culture

After presenting readers with two giants of early twentieth-century thought, Martin counterbalances Einstein and Picasso with a late twentieth-century giant of popular culture. Few would say that Elvis Presley had the same level of creative intelligence as the play's other two towering figures—as good as he was at what he did, other factors, including the rise of television, advances in recording technology, a mingling of black and white cultures domestically and abroad during World War II, and the financial empowerment of teens in the postwar years, had as much to do with his success as his singing and guitar playing did. Still, he is the most widely recognized of the three famous people in this play, and that fact makes popular culture a force that must be given due consideration. The play takes place in a time when mass communication is in its infancy, but the combination of characters suggests that popularity will someday be as important as scientific knowledge or artistic talent.

Martin foreshadows the entry of popular culture into the play with the character of Schmendiman. Arrogant in the same way that Picasso is, feeling that he deserves to be praised because he has invented a product that he considers practical, Schmendiman presents audiences with a useful foil for Einstein and Picasso. He is not an abstract thinker. He works for money and glory, not to fulfill his unique vision. He has no sense of history (thinking that he has invented the dunce cap, which had in fact existed for centuries), but he wants history to remember him. If the play had left popular culture to be represented by just Schmendiman alone, its message would clearly be that intellect is more significant than popularity. By introducing a wildly successful popular figure, however, the play admits that pop culture is a truly important force.

Humor

Having been written by one of the world's most famous comedians, audiences can understandably expect *Picasso at the Lapin Agile* to be a comedy. There are humorous elements to the play, but they are there to help audiences focus on serious, important matters. The humor in this play is scattered, both in placement and in style. It works on different levels. There is abstract, conceptual humor, such as Einstein playing off of the concept of Heisenberg's uncertainty principle by theorizing that the Countess is as likely to meet him in a random place as she is to meet him in the place they both agreed on. There is general nonsense, as when Schmendiman, who has a vaudevillian funny name, says that he has created a building material from asbestos, kitten's paws, and radium. There is cultural humor about the French being haughty and insulting. There is childishness, as when Einstein and Gaston's "Is not!"/"Is too!" debate leads to Germaine and Freddy arguing "Post!" and "Neo!" There are insider jokes, as when Schmendiman says that his product can only be used in New York, San

Francisco, and "Krakatoa, East of Java" (which is the title of a 1969 disaster film—the film itself has been forgotten, but the title lives on as a monument to studio incompetence or arrogance: Krakatoa is *west* of Java). It may seem ironic that the one joke told onstage—the joke Einstein explains about the man who has a pie baked like an "e"—is not funny, but its indecipherable quality fits with the way Martin blends humor and strangeness in this play.

Genius

This play revolves around a number of differing concepts of genius. At the center are the seemingly different talents of Albert Einstein, so commonly recognized as one of history's great intellects that his name has been used as a synonym for "genius," and Pablo Picasso, who is credited with the biggest change of direction in art since the Renaissance. They represent the traditional understanding of the concept, with Einstein representing a math and memory genius and Picasso a genius at artistic creation (though the play disputes these narrow divisions). Adding the figure of Elvis Presley complicates the idea of what a genius is. Though his greatest achievement was fame itself, he would not have achieved that fame without some level of genius.

Looking at these obvious geniuses helps audiences appreciate the lesser geniuses onstage. Suzanne can recognize Picasso's talent and attaches herself to him because of it, just as Sagot's genius is to recognize artistic talent and exploit it for money. Gaston's genius is in memory and in knowing to keep his expectations low. Germaine is intelligent enough to spend her life exploring, from a painter to a street paver to the unappreciated observations of her barkeeper boyfriend, Freddy. Freddy has a working-class form of genius that lets him care for the practical matters that hold up his existence.

Breaking the Fourth Wall

Traditional stages are shaped like a box, with a wall at the back of the stage and walls, or simulated walls, at the sides. Theatrical convention treats the space between the stage and the audience as an invisible wall, keeping the imaginary world separated from the real world. When characters acknowledge the audience's presence or show an awareness of themselves as characters on a stage, it is referred to as "breaking the fourth wall."

The imaginary fourth wall is broken several times in *Picasso at the Lapin Agile*. Early on, Freddy steps into the audience to take a playbill from an audience member, establishing the play's freedom from conventional rules. Later, when the story calls for him to be offstage for a while, Freddy explains that he has to go collect money from someone named Antoine: he turns to the audience to admit that he will be gone from the stage longer than they would think it would take him to collect money, citing theatrical tradition for writing a character out of a scene. Later on, Schmendiman races onstage just as someone says they are taking a historic photo—his hyperawareness of an opportunity to promote himself fits with his egotistical character, but it is not realistic. Breaking the fourth wall violates the reality of the play in order to acknowledge the greater reality of the theatergoing experience.

Episodic Story Structure

Picasso at the Lapin Agile begins with Albert Einstein entering the bar and ends with the cast toasting the new century. In between stands a series of events—characters enter, explain their philosophical positions, and leave without significantly changing the situation. This play does not follow a traditional structure, in which plot points along the way build toward an emotional climax. Each page of the script has an individual discussion that, in general, could be moved from one place to another without disrupting the play's overall design.

Fantasy

Throughout much of this play, Martin keeps a loose hold on reality. Characters interact with the audience, make jokes about future events that they could not know about, walk in and out according to unlikely coincidences, and so forth. Still, the time and place is established as the Lapin Agile, Paris, 1904, and the rules of physics that apply to that setting apply to the stage action.

The reality of the story shifts in the last quarter of the script, with the appearance of a character from the future. At first the visitor says he is there because he felt like traveling through time, but later he tells Picasso that he has come with a message for him. It is at this point that Martin changes the physical rules of their world. The picture above the bar changes, but that could be explained as a manifestation of what Picasso and the visitor imagine. After that, though, a wall opens to reveal the sky. This is no ordinary bar, though it is presented as one throughout most of the play.

The Rule of Threes

Writers, as well as comedians, often structure their narratives to follow the rule of threes. Things happen in stories three times. For most stories, this makes sense: the first occurrence introduces the standard, the second one establishes that a pattern is developing, and the third confirms that the apparent pattern was no coincidence. Going on with any more examples would just be redundant, repeating what the audience already knows.

The characters in *Picasso at the Lapin Agile* are aware to some extent that they are in a play, so when they have two geniuses in their midst they look for a third. Martin takes advantage of this expectation by introducing Schmendiman, who momentarily looks as if he could be the third genius —he is an inventor—but who turns out to be no more than an egotistical fool. His brief appearance serves as a distraction, making audiences forget about a third genius until the visitor, Elvis Presley, arrives.

Einstein before He Was Famous

The year 1904, when *Picasso at the Lapin Agile* takes place, was the last year that Albert Einstein was to toil in obscurity. In 1905, a year that some historians refer to as Einstein's *annus mirabilis*, or "miracle year," he published a series of papers that would redefine physics and mathematics.

The Einstein of history is not the Einstein who is presented in the play, though he is very similar. In real life, as in the play, he was a twenty-five-year-old man who had graduated from Swiss Polytechnic School in 1900 but had been rejected by the academic community. He had submitted his dissertation to the University of Zurich in 1901, but he withdrew it the next year, deciding to figure out his theories on his own while working by day at the Swiss Patent Office. He was married then to his first wife, Mileva Maric, who had been a student with him, and their first son was on the way. It is doubtful that Einstein would have been in Paris in early 1904.

Compare & Contrast

- **1904:** Artists can attain international status by word of mouth and showings of their works at museums and galleries.

1993: Color printing techniques have made it possible to make reproductions of artworks that are reasonably similar to the originals, so that people can enjoy printed copies of the world's great paintings.

Today: Advances in high-definition cameras and high-resolution computer screens have enabled artists to create important works on computers and share them with people around the world.

- **1904:** The Lapin Agile is a tradition in the artists' enclave of Montmartre, having been serving drinks to locals for nearly fifty years.

  1993: The Lapin Agile is world-famous, in part because of the title of one of Picasso's best-known works, *At the Lapin Agile*, which he painted the year after this play takes place.

  Today: Because of the fame brought to it by Picasso's painting and Martin's play, as well as by longevity and marketing, the Lapin Agile is popular with tourists but a little too expensive for artists.

- **1904:** Albert Einstein has not yet published his major works, although he has published a few well-received papers. He is not well known, even in the field of physics.

1993: Einstein is recognized as one of the century's great geniuses and is revered in some circles for being a scientist who stood for peace, a man who made nuclear technology

Today: Einstein is as popular as ever. His unique look is familiar worldwide, in photographs, drawings, and caricatures.

- **1904:** Art is considered a man's pursuit, dominated by male figures like Picasso, Matisse, Ce ´zanne, and John Singer Sargent.

   1993: The art world is starting to be integrated by gender. For instance, this is the first year that the prestigious Turner Prize, presented to a British visual artist under the age of fifty, is presented to a woman, Rachel Whiteread.

   Today: Women are equally represented on art awards juries and on lists of prize winners and finalists, with gender rarely discussed as a consideration.

- **1904:** Popular music is heard in dance halls and concert halls. Sales of sheet music make it possible to play songs at home—songs like

"Give My Regards to Broadway," by George M. Cohan, and "Absinthe Frappe," by Victor Herbert, as well as classical piano songs.

1993: Thirty-seven years after Elvis Presley brought rock and roll to a national audience by appearing on *The Ed Sullivan Show*, rock is by far the most popular style of music in the world.

Today: In America, country music has eclipsed the popularity of rock, though worldwide rock is still more popular.

The four papers that made 1905 his "miracle year" were published that year in the prestigious German journal *Annalen der Physik*. They concerned photoelectric effect (presenting an equation for measuring the behavior of light and electrons, based on a constant that was theorized by Max Planck, who is mentioned in the play); Brownian motion (explaining the movement of pollen grains in water, first studied by biologist Robert Brown in 1827, as being caused by the molecules of the water, which helped advance studies of the size and velocity of atoms); special relativity (concerning the distinctions between relative and absolute perspectives in physics); and mass-energy equivalence (introducing a theory of the conservation of energy with the simple but world-changing equation $E = mc^2$).

The publication of these four papers served as Einstein's doctoral thesis, and they quickly made him one of the most important men in physics. By 1909, he had a chair in theoretical physics at the University of Zurich, a position that was created especially for him. In 1921, he was awarded the Nobel Prize in Physics. By 1922, he traveled the world as one of the most famous scientists on the face of the planet, his face known in magazines in dozens of countries.

Picasso Introduces Cubism

In 1904, Pablo Picasso was at the end of his blue period, a stretch of nearly four years during which he focused on painting with shades of blue. The deep tint of his paint reflected his gloomy outlook on life. Picasso said that he started painting in blue after hearing of the death of Carlos Casagemas, a poet and close friend who had moved with Picasso from Barcelona to Paris in 1901 and killed himself in February of that year. From 1901 to 1904 Picasso became increasingly less academic and more introspective in his art. His subjects during the blue period came from poverty: beggars and prostitutes and drug addicts, as well as several portraits of Casagemas, drawn from memory. He worked to find the reality of his subjects instead of simply dealing in surface appearances. His paintings from the blue period are some of the most famous of his career and therefore some of the most famous paintings of the twentieth century. While his blue period was instrumental in Picasso's formulating theories about art and building an international audience for his work, it was just a prelude to the earthquake he was to release on the art world in the future with the introduction of cubism.

Picasso and Georges Braque are the premier artists of the cubist movement who arose at the end of the first decade of the century. The ideas they worked with came from various sources, ranging from African art to Paul Ce´zanne's flattened, depthless landscapes. The style represents its subjects geometrically, not realistically, emphasizing the segments they are made up of like cubes instead of presenting them with continuous flow. Linear perspective, which was considered one of the great innovations of Western art, is replaced with a vision that shows several aspects of a subject at the same time. The term *cubism* was first used as an insult, a response by painter Henri Matisse and critic Louis Vauxcelles to the boxy vision displayed in Braque's 1908 work *Maisons á l'Estaque*.

The works that brought cubism to international attention were *Maisons á l'Estaque* and Picasso's groundbreaking 1907 painting *Les Demoiselles d'Avignon*, which is revealed to him by the visitor from the future in *Picasso at the Lapin Agile* years before it was actually painted. The effect of cubism on modern art is immeasurable, not only for the artists who painted in this style but also for the way it liberated all artists from strict adherence to realistic norms.

Theater of the Absurd

Martin's *Picasso at the Lapin Agile* owes a great deal of its structure and vision to the dramas produced during the "theater of the absurd" movement that hit its stride in the 1950s and 1960s. The name for this kind of drama was coined by famed theater critic Martin Esslin in his 1962 book of that name. In particular, Esslin examined the works of playwrights Eugène Ionesco, Samuel Beckett, Jean Genet, Arthur Adamov, and Harold Pinter under this category, though others certainly fit his descriptions as well.

The defining characteristic for plays written by these writers was that they worked actively to avoid giving audiences a logical situation. In the best-known absurdist play, Beckett's *Waiting for Godot*, for instance, two tramps wait around a barren set for an unidentified person, a situation that invites audiences to project symbolic meaning onto it in order to find sense where none exists. The play does not follow a narrative path to its conclusion, but instead is built, like avant-garde music, around repeated motifs and phrases. In Ionesco's *Rhinoceros*, reality is subverted when the inhabitants of a French town turn one by one into horned animals onstage.

Of course, Martin, as a comedian, may have written this play drawing from the rich tradition of absurdity in American comedy, from W. C.

Fields and the Marx Brothers to his own early films with Carl Reiner. Without the precedents of the theater of the absurd, the breaks that Martin makes from realism in *Picasso at the Lapin Agile*, with its comic figure Schmendiman and the sudden appearance of the visitor from decades in the future, would create even greater disruptions to his meditation on the nature of modern thought.

Critical Overview

Picasso at the Lapin Agile has been praised by critics in general, though often with some reservations. In a *Newsweek* review of a production of the play in Cambridge, Massachusetts, in 1994, soon after its first run, Jack Kroll declares that it "may be the most sheerly enjoyable play of the season." Caroline Burlingham Ellis reviewed a 2004 run at Beatrice Herford's Vokes Theater in Wayland, Massachusetts, by noting that "Martin's touch is surest in broad comedy. When he reaches for deeper meaning, he is boring." She lauds the actors for their deft over-the-top performances, "not easy in a Steve Martin creation, where it is easy to descend into mere hamming," and decides in the end that "the moments of pure fun are worth the trip."

Martin's name drew attention from national media outlets that another first-time playwright's work might not have garnered. Respected critic Vincent Canby reviewed its 1995 New York debut in the *New York Times*, noting that

> Mr. Martin's play is…. like an extended sketch from the long-ago golden age of "Saturday Night Live." Although there are plenty of good gags, it sometimes seems as if no routine is too obvious or irrelevant to be met at the Lapin Agile.

Canby notes Martin's "passion for ideas, which toward the end of the play comes close to being the sentimental longing of a thinking groupie," but concludes that "when he's on target, which is much of the time, his comedy is very good fun." Fifteen years later, the *New York Times* ran another review of the play when it was in revival in New Jersey. Anita Gates rains praise on the author: "Mr. Martin's authorial voice—with both its intelligence and its silliness—comes through loud and clear throughout this comedy." One of the less impressed critics was Julio Martinez, who reviewed a Los Angeles production for *Variety*, the show-business paper. In particular, Martinez takes exception to Martin's device of adding the contemporary characters Schmendiman and Elvis into a period piece, which he admits was "a quick laugh-inducer" but "ultimately proves an annoying device and a disservice to this often intriguing, humorous social confrontation between two neophyte creative giants." Martinez explains that "both of these characters diffuse the focus and energy from the main characters, leading to a less than edifying or satisfying conclusion to the evening."

Reviewing a 2013 production at the Vienna Theater Company in Vienna, Virginia, Bob Ashby of ShowBizRadio saw the good and the bad of the story, which he labels "a play chock full of monologues." He writes, "Martin's script is uneven, intermittently humorous and tedious." Still, Ashby found enough good in the way the company presented it to recommend it as an evening's entertainment. A 2000 performance won the play honors at the Shellie Awards, honoring the artists and productions at the Central Contra Costa region of California, where it was named best play. It also won Shellies for its director, lead actor, lead actress, and supporting actor. Smaller productions, in general, seem to flourish with Martin's material.

Despite the overall approval of critics, the play stirred controversy in 2009 when it was scheduled for production at La Grande High School in Oregon. One parent objected to the "adult content," leading to a petition drive that caused the play to be cancelled while it was in its third week of rehearsals. Martin himself stepped in and publicly offered funding for the cast to put on the play, but he did not have to: a student group at nearby Eastern Oregon University raised money for the La Grande students to put their production on at the EOU campus.

What Do I Read Next?

- Tom Stoppard's play *Travesties*, originally produced in 1974, tells a similar story of three historic figures (author James Joyce, artist Tristan Tzara, and future Communist party leader V. I. Lenin) who, in one character's flashback, meet during World War I. Although there is no historical record of such a meeting, it could have happened, given that all three lived in Zurich at the same time, making it a more realistic piece than Martin's. *Travesties* is available in a 1994 edition.

- After World War I ended in 1918, Paris became home to a generation of American artists. Best known among these are white writers, such as Ernest Hemingway and F. Scott Fitzgerald. At the same time, Paris served as a haven for a generation of black artists who found freedom from America's racist laws. The complex story of American black artists who found a home in Paris at the time of this play is covered in Tyler Stovall's 1996 book *Paris Noir: African Americans in the City of Light*. Covering the years from World War I to the end of the twentieth century, Stovall discusses the great African American writers, thinkers, and musicians who left their homes in the United States to find refuge in Paris.

- Like Martin, Woody Allen is a comedian who grew beyond stand-up comedy to writing short fiction and films. Although Allen is considered a much more accomplished film writer and director, his early works capture some of the sense of adventure and whimsy of *Picasso at the Lapin Agile*. Allen's one-act play *God*, for instance, presents an ancient Greek drama taking place in Athens, circa 500 BCE, in which a writer and actor discuss the will of the gods with each other, bringing the audience and modern touches like the telephone into the talk. *God* was published in Allen's 1975 collection of humorous writings called *Without Feathers*.

- Martin has published short stories and essays. One of his most memorable pieces is *Shopgirl*, a serious novella about a shy girl who sells gloves at Neiman Marcus in Beverly Hills. This acclaimed story was published as a book in 2000, and in 2005, it was adapted as a movie, written by Martin and starring Martin, Claire Danes, and

Jason Schwartzman.

- Picasso's younger years in Barcelona and Paris are discussed in quite a number of biographies, but one of the best is *Portrait of Picasso as a Young Man*, by acclaimed novelist Norman Mailer, published in 1995.

- The perennial stage play *Bye Bye Birdie*, often performed by school and community theaters, presents, like this play, a thinly veiled version of Elvis Presley. Set in 1958, it presents a satire of American pop culture, then in the throes of Elvismania. The play, written by Michael Stewart, with music by Lee Adams and Charles Strouse, opened on Broadway in 1960 and was adapted into a film in 1963. An edition commemorating a twenty-first-century revival of the play was published in 2005.

- Martin's subject in this play, genius, is the subject of the young-adult novel *Brilliance*, by Marcus Sakey, about a category of children born in 1980 who are each endowed, in their own way, with some form of extraordinary understanding, like mutants of the comic books, but with actual (though exaggerated) human mental abilities. This much lauded book, the first in a series, was published in 2013.

Sources

Ashby, Bob, "Vienna Theater Company *Picasso at the Lapin Agile*," ShowBizRadio, October 25, 2013, http://washingtondc.showbizradio.com/2013/10/revie vtcpicasso/ (accessed August 11, 2014).

Canby, Vincent, "Theater Review: A Fantasy Meeting of Minds," Promenade Theater, in *New York Times*, October 23, 1995, http://www.nytimes.com/1995/10/23/theater/theater-review-a-fantasy-meeting-of-minds.html (accessed August 11, 2014).

"Comedy Central's 100 Greatest Stand-Ups of All Time," Everything2, http://everything2.com/title/Comedy+Central%2527 Ups+of+all+Time (accessed August 14, 2014).

Crabb, Jerome P., "Theater of the Absurd," Theater Database, September 3, 2006, http://www.theatredatabase.com/20th_century/theatr (accessed August 10, 2014).

"Did You Know.... Brownian Motion," in *Einstein Year: 2005*, Institute of Physics, http://www.einsteinyear.org/facts/brownian_motion/ (accessed August 10, 2014).

Elert, Glenn, "Photoelectric Effect," in *Physics Hypertextbook*, 2014, http://physics.info/photoelectric/ (accessed August 21, 2014).

Ellis, Caroline Burlingham, Review of *Picasso at*

the Lapin Agile, Vokes Theatre, in Theater Mirror, 2004, http://www.theatermirror.com/CBEp@lavp.htm (accessed August 11, 2014).

Gates, Anita, "A Couple of Geniuses Walk into a Bar….," Two River Theater Company, in *New York Times*, May 28, 2010, http://www.nytimes.com/2010/05/30/nyregion/30pla module=Search&mabReward=relbias%3Aw&_r=0 (accessed August 11, 2014).

Kroll, Jack, "When Picasso Met Albert," in *Newsweek*, June 20, 1994, http://www.newsweek.com/when-pablomet-albert-189014 (accessed August 11, 2014).

Martin, Steve, "Of Arts and Sciences," in *La Grande (OR) Observer*, March 13, 2009, http://www.lagrandeobserver.com/Opinion/Guest-Columns/Of-arts-andsciences (accessed August 14, 2014).

———, *Picasso at the Lapin Agile and Other Plays*, Grove Press, 1996.

Martinez, Julio, Review of *Picasso at the Lapin Agile*, Wilshire Theatre, in *Variety*, January 22, 1998, http://variety.com/1998/legit/reviews/picasso-at-the-lapinagile-4-1117437047/ (accessed August 11, 2014).

Mason, Dick, "Play Banned at LHS will run at EOU," in *La Grande (OR) Observer*, March 3, 2009, http://www.lagrandeobserver.com/News/Local-

News/Play-banned-at-LHS-will-run-at-EOU (accessed August 14, 2014).

Moffat, Charles Alexander, "Cubism," Art History Archive, http://www.arthistoryarchive.com/arthistory/cubism/ (accessed August 10, 2014).

"Pablo Picasso's Blue Period: 1901 to 1904," PabloPicasso.org, http://www.pablopicasso.org/blue-period.jsp (accessed August 10, 2014).

"Steve Martin Biography," Biography.com, A&E Television Networks, 2014, http://www.biography.com/people/steve-martin-9400755#related-video-gallery (accessed August 11, 2014).

"Steve Martin Biography," IMDb, 2014, http://www.imdb.com/name/nm0000188/bio?ref_=nm_dyk_qt_sm#quotes (accessed August 11, 2014).

"2001—Twenty Second Annual Shellie Awards," Lesher Center for the Arts website, http://www.lesherartscenter.org/shellie-awards-21-25/ (accessed August 11, 2014).

Further Reading

Einstein, Albert, *Ideas and Opinions*, Broadway Books, 1995.

> There are many good biographies of Einstein, but this collection of his most popular writings, spanning his lifetime and edited by Einstein himself for its first publication in 1954, is one of the great texts of the twentieth century.

Ferreira, Pedro, *The Perfect Theory: A Century of Geniuses and the Battle over General Relativity*, Houghton Mifflin Harcourt, 2014.

> This is an engaging telling of the history of the theory, chronicling its weaknesses and its strengths and explaining its overall control over physics of the twentieth century.

Franck, Dan, *Bohemian Paris: Picasso, Modigliani, Matisse, and the Birth of Modern Art*, Grove Press, 1998.

> Franck offers an extensive look at what life was like around the Lapin Agile at the time when the play takes place. The book is written in engaging language that makes the story a compelling read.

Martin, Steve, *Born Standing Up: A Comic's Life*,

Scribner, 2007.

> Reading about the progression of Martin's life and career in his own words gives readers an understanding of what the intellectual figures presented in *Picasso at the Lapin Agile* mean to him, giving the play a richer context.

McCully, Marilyn, *Picasso in Paris: 1900–1907*, Vendome Press, 2011.

> Everything a person reading this play would want to know about the actuality of the painter's situation is covered in this extensively researched, focused biography that makes clear why Martin chose this time and place for his meeting of minds.

Suggested Search Terms

Steve Martin

Steve Martin AND play Steve Martin AND Picasso at the Lapin Agile Steve Martin AND Einstein AND Picasso Einstein AND Picasso AND Elvis Presley Picasso AND Lapin Agile Einstein AND Paris

Elvis Presley AND time travel Lapin Agile AND famous Einstein AND cubism

Steve Martin AND modernism

CPSIA information can be obtained
at www.ICGtesting.com
Printed in the USA
LVHW051145220722
724085LV00005B/666